Cursed!

Biblical Curses, Sins and Acts That Constitute a Curse

By Pastor Donna Morse

Proverbs 26:2

As the bird by wandering, as the swallow by flying, so the curse causeless shall not come.

For every effect, there is a cause…

It is recommended that your print this document for a more enjoyable reading and learning experience.

Copyright Notice

Legal Notice

Contents

Introduction
Curses Have A Beginning

Definition of A Curse...6

Salvation (**IMPORTANT**: Must Read This Section)....................10

Be Filled With The Holy Spirit...18

Are You Cursed? Checklist...25

Biblical Curses Reference List...32

Answers to Frequently Asked Questions..................................37

Declare a Thing..44

Time and Effort..46

Reality of Life Today in the Earth and God's Remedy........................47

It Is Time For Us To See Our Lifes Transformed 49

Curses Have a Beginning

Proverbs c.26 v2:

As the bird by wandering, as the swallow by flying, so the curse causeless shall not come.

For every effect, there is a cause

Curses can't just make their home without an entry point; words, covenants, sin and behaviors can be entry points that provide places for curses to land and remain until they are dealt with and broken.

Many Christians attend church regularly and strive with all their hearts to lead a godly victorious life. However, no matter how hard they try or how much counseling they receive, nothing seems to help and the result is always the same -- they lead a defeated life and the cycles return time and time again. Many are plagued with physical illness, suicide, alcoholism, divorce, incest, and poverty. Eventually they give up on God and fall away always wondering what went wrong.

These problems may result from a number of factors, but one of the most overlooked reasons is the operation of a curse on the person's life or family (generational curse) that has never been dealt with or broken. This is one of the most neglected areas in the life of a Christian today. The church has failed in teaching this very important topic, which would bring freedom and victory to so many of God's people.

Some question the significance of "sins of the fathers" and the effect they have (or don't have) on succeeding generations. The first biblical mention of the iniquity of fathers affecting their children and grandchildren is in The Ten Commandments, where God says regarding idol worship,

Exodus c20 v5:

You shall not bow down to them nor serve them. For I, the Lord your God am a jealous God, visiting the iniquity of the fathers upon the children to the third and fourth generation of those who hate Me.

You may be saying to yourself right now that you are not an idol worshiper. Let's stop and think about twenty-first-century idols:

4

Money, possessions, drugs, overspending, entertainment-hungry, success-driven, alcohol, career driven, we even worship church leaders and their ministry.

In Deuteronomy chapters 27 and 28 lists the curses and blessings of God. Obedience brings blessings and disobedience brings curses. You should take time to read these chapters and as you do you will begin to come into the knowledge of things you have never known or seen before in the Word of God! God's Word is conditional – If you do what His Word says to do – then God will do what He promises He will do!!

When a curse is in operation in your life it has a purpose:

That purpose is to pursue you, overtake you, until you are destroyed.
Deuteronomy c28 v45-46: says it this way:

Moreover all these curses shall come upon you and pursue and overtake you, until you are destroyed, because you did not obey the voice of the Lord your God, to keep His commandments and His statutes, which He commanded you.

And they shall be upon you for a sign and a wonder, and on your descendants forever.

You can be destroyed by what you don't know! The road to hell is paved with ignorance! I am sure you all have heard the saying, "sticks and bones may break my bones, but words will never hurt me." That is a lie – word curses can destroy you!

Satan is so deceptive and makes things look harmless when in reality they are deadly!

The good news is that you can be Free!

Definition of a Curse

Exactly what is a curse? First, let's look at the dictionary definition:

Curse - (n) a prayer or invocation for harm or injury to come upon one; evil or misfortune that comes as if in response to imprecation or as retribution; a cause of great harm or misfortune

Curse - (v) to use profanely insolent language against, blaspheme; to call upon divine or supernatural power to send injury upon; to execrate in fervent and often profane terms; to bring great evil upon, afflict

When a curse is placed on someone, the purpose is to cause injury and destruction - sometimes to the point of death.

The Scriptures of the Old Testament are full of references to curses. The New Testament tells us that Jesus Christ came and died on the cross, conquering Satan, so that we can be set free from curses. *(Galatians 3:13)* Jesus gave His servants the power in His name to break curses.

Why then are Christians still so defeated and afflicted by curses? The answer is ignorance. You can't fight a battle you don't see or know exists. You cannot defeat an enemy when you don't even know he is attacking you. God's Word says the following:

My people are destroyed for lack of knowledge. *(Hosea 4:6)*

Therefore my people have gone into captivity, because they have no knowledge; their honorable men are famished, and their multitude dried up with thirst. Therefore Sheol has enlarged itself and opened its mouth beyond measure. *(Isaiah 5:13-14)*

For wisdom is a defense as money is a defense, but the excellence of knowledge is that wisdom gives life to those who have it. *(Ecclesiastes 7:12)*

Lest Satan should take advantage of us; for we are not ignorant of his devices. *(2 Corinthians 2:11)*

6

The Scriptures clearly state that God's people will suffer and eventually be taken into captivity if they continue in ignorance and sin. This applies in the case of curses. Far too, often, Christians do not realize that curses have been placed on their lives. Thus, they cannot deal with them, but they wonder why they continually suffer afflictions as they do.

The most common argument from people is: "I don't believe God would hold me responsible for something I don't know about. I don't believe God would allow a curse to come on my life when I did not know I was doing something wrong.

Dear brothers and sisters, God does hold you accountable for everything that is in His Word. He has given us ample information throughout the Bible. Every one of us has access to a Bible. We are without any excuse. Let's look at these Scriptures:

If a person sins, and commits any of these things which are forbidden to be done by the commandments of the Lord, though he does not know it, yet he is guilty and shall bear his iniquity. *(Leviticus 5: 17)*

For it is a people of no understanding; therefore He who made them will not have mercy on them, and He who formed them will show them no favor. *(Isaiah 27:11)*

Hear, 0 earth! Behold, I will certainly bring calamity on this people; the fruit of their thoughts, because they have not heeded My words, nor My law, but rejected it. *(Jeremiah 6:19)*

My people are destroyed for lack of knowledge. Because you have rejected knowledge, I also will reject you from being priest for Me; because you have forgotten the law of your God, I also will forget your children. *(Hosea 4:6)*

If you do not read and study God's Word, then you are rejecting knowledge. The consequences of this sin are grave indeed. However we do serve a merciful God who is quick to forgive us when we repent and we have the Holy Spirit who dwells in us to help us.

Are you experiencing unsolved problems in your life, your family, or your church? Perhaps the source of these problems is an unbroken curse. Pray and ask the Holy Spirit to reveal to you any curses that may be in operation in your life. He will be faithful to do so.

However, when He, the Spirit of truth, has come, He will guide you into all truth; for He will not speak on His own authority, but whatever He hears He will speak; and He will tell you things to come. *(John 16:7-13)*

Unfortunately, some Christians believe that they don't have to bother with curses at all. They assume that God will handle them. However, Jesus specifically told us that He has given us authority over Satan and his kingdom. *(Luke 10:19; Mark 16:17; and 2 Corinthians 7:1)* With authority comes responsibility! It is our responsibility to break any curses sent onto us. Jesus Christ gave us the power to do so, and He expects us to use the authority given to us in His name.

There Are Conditions With God

If you want to receive all the blessings that God has promised in His Word then you must give Him your life with a sincere heart and you must live according to His Word.

There are no short cuts with God. You will not be able to stand in your freedom if you don't know the one who gave it to you!

God is faithful to do what He promises if you will do what is required of you!

Salvation is your first step -- now walk toward Him!

Salvation

If you died today, where would you spend eternity?

This is the most important question anyone could ever ask you and if you don't know then you haven't made Jesus Christ Lord of your life and you will spend eternity in Hell!

Salvation means deliverance, victory, prosperity and welfare and you can't have one without the other!

In *John 3: 1-7*, Jesus told Nicodemus, who was a sincere "religious" leader:

- **You must be born again.**

- **You need a new nature.**

- **You must experience a spiritual rebirth**

- **No man can get to Heaven without being born again!**

This is what God says about the condition of every lost person:

- By nature all men are spiritually dead
  (Colossians 2:13)

- The unbeliever walks according to the lusts of the flesh and the carnal mind
  (Ephesians 2:3)

- By nature all men are children of wrath
  (Ephesians 2:3)

- The unbeliever is a prisoner to the law of sin and death
  (Romans 8:2; John 5:24; John 8:34)

- By nature all men are children of the devil
  (1 John 3:10)

- The unbeliever is an enemy of God
  (Romans 5:10)

- Every unsaved person is in the family of Satan
  (Ephesians 2:1-3)

- The unbeliever is alienated (cut off) from the life of God
  (Ephesians 4:18)

- By nature all men are cursed with Adam's sin nature
  (Romans 5:12)

- The unbeliever is far from God and without hope
  (Ephesians 2: 12-13)

- By nature all men are children of disobedience
  (Ephesians 2:2)

- The unbeliever is guilty before God and living under God's wrath
  (Romans 3:19; John 3:36)

- The unbeliever has his mind blinded and his understanding clouded with darkness
  (Ephesians 4:18; 2 Corinthians 4:4)

- Every unsaved person is living in the kingdom of darkness under Satan's lordship and influence
  (Colossians 1:13; Acts 26:18)

- Every unsaved person has the nature of the devil
  (John 8:44)

- Every unsaved person has demon activity working in his life
  (Ephesians 2:2)

Some of the effects of sin in man:

- Sin dulls man's ears
  (Acts 28:27)

- Sin darkens his eyes
  (Ephesians 4:18)

- Sin damns his soul
  (Ezekiel 18:4)

- Sin devours his intellect
  (1Corinthians 2:14)

- Sin defiles his tongue
  (Romans 3:13-14)

- Sin deceives his heart
  (Jeremiah 17:9)

- Sin diverts his feet
  (Isaiah 53:6)

In salvation we stop trying to make ourselves acceptable to God, and by faith we accept Him as Lord.

God has provided the remedy for the sin problem at the cross. At Calvary, God's Son Jesus cancelled the power of sin and made spiritual life available to spiritually dead men.

You may be asking yourself right now ---- what was done for me when Jesus Christ went to the cross and died over two thousand years ago? Everything was done for you!

Look what was done on the cross just for you!!

Jesus accomplished defeat of Satan. The cross cancelled Satan's legal claim over the human race
(Hebrews 2:14-15; Colossians 2:14-17; John 12:31-32)

Jesus opened the way of personal access to God for every believer
(Matthew 27:51; Ephesians 2: 14-18; Hebrews 10: 19-22)

Jesus accomplished God's plan of salvation, making righteousness available for mankind
(Hebrews 9: 12-15, 26; Matthew 26:28; Colossians 1:14; Ephesians 1:7)

Jesus canceled the power of sin. Sin's penalty was paid for and sin's power was broken eternally
(1 Corinthians 16:54-58; Romans 6:1-23)

Jesus purchased bodily healing for the sick and afflicted
(1 Peter 2:24; Isaiah 53:4-5; Matthew 8:17)

At the cross Jesus Christ was our:

Sin bearer
(Matthew 1:21)

Curse bearer and curse breaker
(Galatians 3:13)

Sickness bearer
(Matthew 8:17)

All of the curse (sin and the effects of sin) was placed on Jesus so that all of the blessings might come on us!

Jesus took:

- Our sin
- Our fear and oppression
- Our rejection
- Our sickness
- Our curse
- Our disease
- Our poverty
- Our spiritual death

Jesus gave us:

- Forgiveness and righteousness
- Peace and a sound mind
- Freedom from rejection
- Healing and health
- Abraham's blessings
- Physical wholeness and well being
- Prosperity
- Eternal life

Jesus Christ took everything and gave us everything on the cross of Calvary!

Some people think because they do certain things that means they are saved, but NOT necessarily!

Salvation has nothing to do with:

- Church membership
- Water baptism
- Doing good deeds and live our best and work our way into Heaven
- Doing penance for our sins
- Keeping the Ten Commandments
- Going to church or saying our prayers
- Education or how many degrees you have
- Good Works
- Observing religious duties
- Living life by the golden rule and helping others
- Tithing and giving money to the church
- Attempting to make up for our sins through good works or by giving up certain things
- Reading or memorizing the Bible
- Being a good, honest citizen
- Taking communion
- Being cultured, refined, or acting religious

If you have trusted in any of these things you have a false salvation and none of these things can save you!

We do not need religion we need a true spiritual heart transplant! It is impossible for us to change our nature – only God can supernaturally change our nature!

The salvation experience is a new creation from Heaven through a direct operation of the word of God and the Holy Spirit upon our lives – spiritually changing us completely and making us righteous (right standing with God) new creatures in Christ!!

Salvation is a divine act that changes us from the family of Satan to the family of God – from being a child of the devil to becoming a child of God, from having the nature of Satan to having the nature of God!

The instant you repent and by faith take Jesus as your Lord, you are born again – you are taken out of the kingdom of darkness (Satan's kingdom) and put into the kingdom of light (God's Kingdom).

Two conditions for every sinner to be born again:

- Repentance
- Personal faith in the Lord Jesus Christ

What repentance is and is not:

Repentance is not human remorse or feeling sorry for the consequences of your sins. Repentance is not self reformation or trying to turn over a new leaf.

True Repentance is a complete change of heart, change of mind, and change of attitude, that causes you to turn away from sin and go in a new direction and turn to God for salvation. And the result will be a changed lifestyle!!!

Changes You Will Experience:

- Change in lifestyle
- Change in the places you go to
- Change of friends and associations
- Change in your speech
- Change in your habits

Salvation and this new birth produces a transformed life, the way you think, talk, live, and act will be changed!!

Now let's begin your journey to a new way of life!!

I would like to tell you that when you come to Christ that everything will be easy and you won't have to go through anything or face things in your life, but that just isn't the way that it is!

Receiving salvation is the easy part --- the ongoing call to "work out (our) salvation with fear and trembling" is the challenge!!

Work out means "to work fully until finished." Everything in your life will not be fixed instantly, but as you being to understand your spiritual foundation you will have the capacity to deal with unresolved past issues and walk in all that Jesus Christ has done for you!! If you want change in your life that change will have to being with you!

Romans 10:9-10, 13 says:
That if you confess with your mouth the Lord Jesus and believe in your heart that God has raised Him from the dead, you will be saved. For with the heart one believes unto righteousness, and with the mouth confession is made unto salvation. For "whoever calls on the name of the Lord shall be saved."

Salvation Prayer:

If you are sincere and are ready to accept Jesus Christ as your Lord and Savior pray this prayer from your heart.

Dear Heavenly Father, I come to you in the name of Jesus Christ. I realize that Jesus is the only Way, the Truth, and the Life; and is the only Mediator between You and man. I acknowledge to You that I am a sinner. I believe that Your only begotten son Jesus Christ shed His precious blood on the cross, died for my sins, and rose again on the third day. I am truly sorry for the sins which I have committed against You, and therefore, I am willing to repent (turn away from my sins). Have mercy on me, a sinner. Cleanse me, and forgive me of my sins.

Right now I confess Jesus as the Lord of my life and open the door of my heart and ask Him to come in and give me a new life with purpose and destiny. I want to serve you Lord and obey all your ways. This very moment I receive and believe that according to

His Word, right now I am born again. Thank You, Jesus, for coming into my heart and life and hearing my prayer. I am truly grateful for Your grace which has led me to repentance and has saved me from my sins. Lord Jesus, please transform my life so that I may bring glory and honor to You alone and not to myself.

I ask all of this in the name of my Lord and Savior, Jesus Christ.
Amen.

I rejoice and thank God with you for having accepted the gift of salvation. You are now a follower of Jesus Christ!

Welcome to the family of God!

BE FILLED WITH THE HOLY SPIRIT

And do not be drunk with wine, in which is dissipation; but be <u>filled</u> with the Spirit **(Ephesians 5:18)**

THE HOLY SPIRIT - WHO IS HE?

The Holy Spirit is the third member of the Trinity **(Matthew 28:19)**

The Holy Spirit is on the earth to help us live victoriously. God the Father is in Heaven and the Lord Jesus is at the Father's right hand. It is only the Holy Spirit who is here on the earth to help us. He is our helper, but He will not help somebody who doesn't want to be helped. We must ask Him for His help every day.

The Holy Spirit is God's *agent on the earth* continuing the ministry of Jesus. We need to operate through Him in order to get things done.

The Holy Spirit *is a person*, with personality traits. He can *be grieved, lies to, and insulted. He has a voice and a mind.*

The Holy Spirit knows the *past, the present, and the future.*

- **He is omniscient - all knowing**
- **He is omnipotent - all powerful**
- **He is omnipresent - everywhere present at the same time**

THE HOLY SPIRIT – WHAT DOES HE DO?

The Holy Spirit is our comforter **(John 14:26)**. We don't have to live in despair, discouragement, or depression. Every day, 24 hours a day, we have the Spirit of God as our indwelling friend and comforter.

The Holy Spirit is our prayer partner **(Romans 8:26-27)**

The Holy Spirit is our teacher. He will give us revelation and understanding of God's word.

The Holy Spirit warns us and protects us from danger and harm.

This includes accidents, calamity, deceptive people, <u>and other dangers. His protection covers not only</u> our own lives, but our family and children also.

The Holy Spirit gives us instructions **(Acts 13:2)**.
We are soldiers in God's end-time army, so we can expect orders from the Holy Spirit for the work of God's service.

The Holy Spirit leads us and guides us **(Romans 8:14, Acts 16:6-7)**.

YOU SHALL RECEIVE POWER

It is not God's plan or intention that only the five ministries listed in **Ephesians 4:11** - apostles, prophets, teachers, pastors, and evangelists – heal the sick, deliver the oppressed, work the works of Christ, and set the captives free. *God appointed all Christians to carry out these works*. Jesus promised, "You will receive the power of God!" **(Acts 1:8)**

God did not design us to be born again and spend the rest of our lives sitting in church warming the pews! Too many Christians come to church to watch the preacher perform miracles, as if only the five ministries of Ephesians 4:11 have supernatural gifts.

God wants every born-again Christian to be supernaturally equipped and anointed to destroy the works of the devil – every born-again factory worker, homemaker, executive, and student.

Acts 1:8 says, "You shall receive power."

Acts 2:4 says, "They ……..began."

When we are baptized in the Holy Spirit and receive the Bible experience of <u>speaking in tongues, then our life in the supernatural begins.</u>

- We begin to heal the sick.
- We begin to cast out devils.
- We begin to preach the gospel in the power of God.
- We begin to witness for Christ.
- We begin to flow in a new dimension of praise and worship.
- We receive revelation knowledge of God's word.
- We experience righteousness, peace, and joy in the Holy Spirit.
- We begin to destroy the works of the devil in the power of the Spirit.
- We begin to set the captives free.
- We resist Satan and overcome the flesh.
- We begin to move in the gifts of the Spirit.

HOW TO RECEIVE THE BAPTISM IN THE HOLY SPIRIT

Our Lord Jesus Christ is the baptizer in the Holy Spirit. We can come to Jesus with childlike faith and ask Him to baptize us in the Holy Spirit.

Matthew 3:11
Mark 1:8
Luke 3:16
John 1:33

Following salvation, God's gift for all believers is the baptism in the Holy Spirit. Salvation is God's gift to the sinner, which involves being born of the Spirit **(John 3:3-5)**. The Holy Spirit is God's gift to His children and involves being baptized in the Spirit **(Acts 1:5)**.

Luke 11:13
John 7: 37-39
Acts 2:38-39

When we receive the baptism in the Holy Spirit, we will receive the Bible evidence of speaking in tongues.

And they were all filled with the Holy Spirit and began to speak with other tongues, as the Spirit gave them utterance. **(Acts 2:4)**

Notice that *"all" believers were filled* with the Holy Spirit and *"all"* spoke in other tongues. The New Testament record clearly shows that being baptized in the Holy Spirit and speaking in tongues are connected together.

- On the day of Pentecost, the 120 believers were filled with the Spirit and spoke in tongues. **(Acts 2:4)**

Receiving the baptism in the Holy Spirit always carries with it the evidence of speaking in tongues. We must remove any barriers to receiving the baptism in the Holy Spirit, such as:

- **Lack of knowledge or wrong doctrine**
- **Pride, especially religious pride**
- **Fear**
- **Our natural mind, which can get in the way and become a blockage**

PURPOSE OF SPEAKING IN TONGUES

Speaking in tongues is a supernatural means of direct communication with God **(1 Corinthians 14:2)**

Speaking in tongues causes us to speak mysteries, "divine secrets," and "hidden wisdom" to God. Praying in tongues is the believer's "hotline" to Heaven.

Romans 8:26
1 Corinthians 2:6-14
1 Corinthians 14:2

When we speak or pray in tongues, our minds are unfruitful and understand nothing. Our minds are bypassed and detached, and our spirits are in control. We are praying in tongues by the Holy Spirit out of our spirits and talking mysteries to God. Jesus said that believers have the privilege and the ability to know the mysteries of the Kingdom of God. **(Matthew 13:11).**

Speaking in tongues is a God-given way to <u>edify ourselves</u>
(1 Corinthians 14:4, Jude 20-21).

- **Praying in the Holy Spirit is a supernatural means of building up our spirit. To edify means to build up, strengthen, restore, replenish with spiritual power, and construct. Praying in tongues builds up our inner man, and helps us to love God and stay on fire for Him. When we don't pray in tongues, our heart grows cold.**

When we speak in tongues, we have the <u>God-given ability to interpret what we have spoken in the Spirit</u> **(1 Corinthians 14:13)**. We can pray to interpret in English what we have spoken in tongues.

Speaking in tongues <u>energizes</u> and activates our human spirit with the life of God.

1 Corinthians 14:14-15
Proverbs 20:27
John 7:38

Praying in tongues releases living water from our spirit man and energizes our spirit with strength and spiritual power.

Praying in tongues is a decision of the will, and therefore <u>brings our will into line with the will of God</u>. **(1 Cor. 14:15; Romans 8:27).** When we pray in tongues, we put our will in subjection to the will of God.

STEPS TO RECEIVE THE BAPTISM IN THE HOLY SPIRIT

- We repent and acknowledge Jesus as our Lord and Savior.
- We ask Jesus to baptize us with the Holy Spirit.
- We believe we receive gifts of the Holy Spirit because we asked in faith. (Luke 11:13).
- As an act of our faith, we <u>open our mouths and start speaking out the new language that God gives us.</u>

<u>We must open our mouths and speak out in tongues (not in English)</u> the language that the Holy Spirit gives us. It is our voice and our mouth, but we are giving voice to the utterance of the Holy Spirit. We must be bold and fluent, not keeping our mouth shut (**Acts 2:4; Psalm 81:10**), nor praising the Lord in English, because we can't speak two languages at the same time. We must speak syllables, the sounds from our spirit by faith, not listening to the devil or our minds. The devil will put negative thoughts into our minds and tell us, "It's just 'mumbo jumbo' or 'gibberish.' Give no place to the devil!

Receive the infilling of the Holy Spirit and let Him take control over your life. God demands a high and holy standard of life, but He has also provided the means to produce it... Walk in the Spirit, and you shall not fulfill the lust of the flesh (**Galatians 5:16**).

We must turn from all known sin to a daily reliance on the Holy Spirit if we are to have the evidence and fullness and fruit of the Holy Spirit in our lives.

WHY NOT BEGIN TODAY?

PRAYER

Heavenly Father, I plead the blood of Jesus Christ over me and I thank You for the most wonderful gift of salvation. Jesus You promised me another gift, the gift of the infilling of the Holy Spirit. I ask You Jesus, to fill me with Your Holy Spirit and fire now just as you filled Your disciples on the day of Pentecost. Jesus I want to be a disciple of Yours filled with the power of the Holy Spirit.

I forgive all those who have ever caused me pain, trauma, shock, harm, rejection, or shame and I ask You to forgive them. I ask You to forgive me for holding a judgment against them.

Jesus, breathe in me Your Holy Spirit now…I lift up my hands unto You Jesus worshiping and praising You in the Spirit. I give thanks, praise, and glory to You forever with all my heart. Jesus I thank You that You have granted me out of the rich treasury of Your glory to be strengthened and reinforced with mighty power of my inner man by the Holy Spirit!

THANK YOU LORD JESUS THAT YOU HAVE FILLED ME WITH YOUR HOLY SPIRIT AND FIRE --- I RECEIVE IT NOW IN THE NAME OF JESUS!

NOW GIVE HIM PRAISE!

Are You Cursed?

✓ Checklist

Biblical Curses, Sins and Acts That Constitute a Curse…

If you answer yes to any of the following items there is a high probability you have a curse operating in your life…

Note: The supporting scripture is listed with each item. A list of curses as stated in the Bible is provided for reference.

1.   Have you ever attempted to turn anyone away from God?
      (Deuteronomy 13: 6-9)

2.   Have you been involved in witchcraft?
      (Exodus 22:18)

3.   Have you sacrificed anything to false gods?
      (Exodus 22:20)

4.   Have you been responsible for letting your animal bring death to someone
      when you knew it was out of control and yet did nothing about it?
      (Exodus 21:29)

5.   Have you ever caused the unborn to die? (also abortion)
      (Exodus 21: 22,23)

6.   Have you ever cursed your parents? (to abuse verbally)
      (Exodus 21:17)

7.   Have you ever kidnapped anyone?
      (Exodus 21:16; Deuteronomy 24:7)

8.   Have you ever struck your parents when you were a child?
      (Exodus 21:15)

9.   Have you ever deliberately attacked someone intending to kill them?
      (Exodus 21:14)

10.   Have you ever murdered someone?
      (Exodus 21:12)

11.   Were you born out of an incestuous union?
      (Genesis 19: 36-38)

12.   Are you an illegitimate child? (curse in effect for 10 generations – Family
      curse)
      (Deuteronomy 23:2)

13.   Have you ever rewarded evil for good?
      (Proverbs 17:13)

14.   Do you follow horoscopes?
      (Deuteronomy 17: 2-5)

15.   Do you refuse to fight spiritual warfare for the Lord?
      (Jeremiah 48:10; 1 Kings 20: 35-42)

16.   Have you done the work of the Lord deceitfully?
      (Jeremiah 48:10)

17.   Have you put your trust in man and not in the Lord?
      (Jeremiah 17:5)

18.   Are you a prideful person? (abomination to God – God hates pride)
      (Psalms 119:21)

19.   Have you ever committed adultery? (extra-marital sex)
      (Deuteronomy 22:22-27, Job 24:15-18)

20.   Have you ever taken money to murder someone?
      (Deuteronomy 27:25)

21.   Have you ever smote (to strike heavily; to kill by striking; to affect as if by a heavy blow) your neighbor secretly?
      (Deuteronomy 27:24)

22.   Have you ever had sex with your sister? (incest)
      (Deuteronomy 27:22)

23.   Have you ever had sex with an animal? (beastiality)
      (Deuteronomy 27:21; Exodus 22:19)

24.   Have you had sex before marriage?
      (Deuteronomy 22:13-21)

25.   Do you discipline your children or do you honor them above God?
      (1 Samuel 2:17; 27-36)

26.   Have you taught anyone to be rebellious against the Lord?
       (Jeremiah 28:16, 17)

27.   Have you refused to warn someone of sin when the Lord has told you to do
       so?
       (Ezekiel 3:18-21)

28.   Do you work seven days a week and refuse to observe the Sabbath day of
       rest?
       (Exodus 31:14; Numbers 15:32-36)

29.   Have you had sex with your father's wife? (incest)
       (Deuteronomy 27:20)

30.   Have you ever oppressed a stranger, widow, or the fatherless?
       (Deuteronomy 27:19; Exodus 22:22-24)

31.   Have you ever taken advantage of the blind? (wrong attitude toward the
       helpless)
       (Deuteronomy 27:18)

32.   Have you been an adulterous woman? (harlot, prostitute)
       (Numbers 5:27)

33.   Have you ever cursed or mistreated the Jewish people?
       (Deuteronomy 27:26; Genesis 27:29, 12:3; Numbers 24:9)

34.   Have you ever willingly deceived anyone? (especially those who deceive
       God's people)
       (Joshua 9:23, Jeremiah 48:10, Malachi 1:14, Genesis 27:12)

35.   Have you ever been disobedient to the Lord's commandments? (His Word)
       (Deuteronomy 11:28, Daniel 9:11, Jeremiah 11:3)

36.   Have you ever worshipped or esteemed something or someone above the
       living God including secret societies?
       (Jeremiah 44:8, Deuteronomy 29:19, 5:8,9, Exodus 20: 3-5)

37. Do you keep or own cursed objects? (statues of demon gods and jewelry with occultic symbols, etc)
(Deuteronomy 7:25-26, Joshua 6:18)

38. Do you refuse to come to the Lord's help? (fight for the Lord)
(Judges 5:23)

39. Is your home a godly home that lives according to God's Word? (if God's blessing is not there, the curse is)
(Proverbs 3:33)

40. Do you refuse to give to the poor and divert your attention from the misery they suffer?
(Proverbs 28:27)

41. The earth by reason of man's disobedience (shows what happens because of sin)
(Isaiah 24:3-6)

42. Jerusalem is a curse to all nations if Jews rebel against God. (statement)
(Jeremiah 26:6)

43. Do you steal, or swear falsely by the Lord's name?
(Zechariah 5:4)

44. If you are a minister, have you failed to give glory to God? (even the blessings will be cursed.)
(Malachi 3:9; Revelation 1:6)

45. Have you ever robbed God of tithes and offerings?
(Malachi 3:9; Revelation 1:6-9, Haggai 1:6-9)

46. Do you listen more to your wife than to God?
(Genesis 3:17)

47. Do you lightly esteem your parents? (dishonoring father and mother)
(Deuteronomy 27:16)

48.   Have you made any graven images? (one of the primary causes of curses is turning away from God to the cult or occult)
(Deuteronomy 27:15, Exodus 20:4 Deuteronomy 5:8)

49.   Have you willingly cheated someone out of his or her property? (mistreating your neighbor)
(Deuteronomy 27:17)

50.   Have you ever sacrificed a human being?
(Leviticus 20:2)

51.   Have you self-appointed yourself a prophet and given forth prophetic words, even with names and dates, which haven't come to pass?
(Deuteronomy 18:19-22)

52.   Have you ever participated in séances and fortune telling?
(Leviticus 20:6)

53.   Have you ever been in a homosexual or lesbian relationship?
(Leviticus 20:13)

54.   Have you ever had sexual intercourse during menstruation?
(Leviticus 20:18)

55.   Have you ever talked to the dead or told someone's fortune?
(Leviticus 20:27)

56.   Have you ever blasphemed (cursed) the Lord's Name?
(Leviticus 24:15, 16)

57.   Are you carnally minded? (fleshly)
(Romans 8:6)

58.   Have you ever had oral or anal sex?
(Genesis 19:13, 24, 25)

59.   Do you have rebellious children?
(Deuteronomy 21:18-21)

60.   Have you ever rebelled against a pastor appointed by God?
        (Deuteronomy 17:12)

61.   Have you cursed those that rule over you?
        (1 Kings 2:8, 9; Exodus 22:28)

Biblical Curses

List Of Curses As Referenced In The Bible

1. Those who attempt to turn anyone away from the Lord.
    (Deuteronomy 13:6-9)

2. Those involved in witchcraft.
    (Exodus 22:18)

3. Those who sacrifice to false gods.
    (Exodus 22:20)

4. Those who do not prevent death.
    (Exodus 21:29)

5. Those who cause the unborn to die.
    (Exodus 21: 22,23)

6. Those who curse their parents.
    (Exodus 21:17)

7. Kidnappers
    (Exodus 21:16; Deuteronomy 24:7)

8. Children who strike their parents.
    (Exodus 21:15)

9. To murder indirectly.
    (Exodus 21:14)

10. Murderers.
    (Exodus 21:12)

11.   Children born from incestuous unions.
      (Genesis 19:36-38)

12.   Illegitimate children (curse of bastard children)
      (Deuteronomy 23:2)

13.   Those who reward evil for good.
      (Proverbs 17:13)

14.   Those who follow horoscopes.
      (Deuteronomy 17:2-5)

15.   Those who do the work of the Lord deceitfully.
      (Jeremiah 48:10)

16.   Those who trust in man instead of the Lord, depending on the flesh instead
      of the Spirit.
      (Jeremiah 17:5)

17.   The Proud.
      (Psalm 119:21)

18.   Adulterers.
      (Job 24:15-18; Deuteronomy 22: 22-27)

19.   Those who take money to slay the innocent.
      (Deuteronomy 27: 25)

20.   Those who smite their neighbors secretly.
      (Deuteronomy 27:24)

21.   Him who lies with his sister.
      (Deuteronomy 27:22)

22.   Him who lies with any beast.
      (Deuteronomy 27:21; Exodus 22:19)

23.   Women who keep not their virginity until they are married.
      (Deuteronomy 22:13-21)

24. Parents who do not discipline their children, but honor them above God
    (I Samuel 2:17; 27-36)

25. Those who teach rebellion against the Lord.
    (Jeremiah 28: 16, 17)

26. Those who refuse to warn them of sin.
    (Ezekial 3:18-21)

27. Those who defile the sabbath.
    (Exodus 31:14; Numbers 15:32-36)

28. Him who lies with his father's wife.
    (Deuteronomy 27:20)

29. Those who oppress strangers, widows or fatherless.
    (Deuteronomy 27: 19; Exodus 22: 22-24)

30. Those you take advantage of the blind.
    (Deuteronomy 27: 18)

31. An adulterous woman.
    (Numbers 5:27)

32. Those who curse or mistreat Jews.
    (Deuteronomy 27: 26; Genesis 27:29; Genesis 12:3; Numbers 12:9)

33. Those who are willing deceivers.
    (Joshua 9:23; Jeremiah 48:10; Malachi 1:14; Genesis 27:12)

34. Disobedience to the Lord's Commandments.
    (Deuteronomy 11:28; Daniel 9:11; Jeremiah 11: 3)

35. Idolatry.
    (Jeremiah 44:8; Deuteronomy 29:19; Exodus 20:5; Deuteronomy 5:8,9)

36. Those who keep or own cursed objects.
    (Deuteronomy 7:25; Joshua 6:18)

37.   Those who will not fight or are slack in the Lord's battle.
        (Judges 5:23)

38.   House of the wicked.
        (Proverbs 3:33)

39.   He who gives not to the poor.
        (Proverbs 28:27)

40.   The earth by reason of man's disobedience.
        (Isaiah 24: 3-6)

41.   Jerusalem is a curse to all nations if Jews rebel against God.
        (Jeremiah 26:6)

42.   Thieves and those who swear falsely by the Lord's name.
        (Zechariah 5: 3,4)

43.   Ministers and any believer who will not give glory to Christ.
        (Malachi 2:2)

44.   Those who rob God of tithes and offerings and fail to give to His work.
        (Malachi 3:9 Haggai 1: 6-9)

45.   Those who hearken unto their wives rather than God.
        (Genesis 3:17)

46.   Those who lightly esteem their parents.
        (Deuteronomy 27: 16)

47.   Those who make graven images.
        (Deuteronomy 27:15; Exodus 20:4; Deuteronomy 5:8)

48.   Those who willfully cheat people out of their property.
        (Deuteronomy 27: 17)

49.   Those who sacrifice human beings.
        (Leviticus 20:2)

50.   False prophets.
       (Deuteronomy 18: 19-22)

51.   Participants in seances and fortune telling.
       (Leviticus 20:6)

52.   Homosexual and lesbian relationships.
       (Leviticus 20:13)

53.   Sexual intercourse during menstruation.
       (Leviticus 20: 18)

54.   Necromancers and fortunetellers.
       (Leviticus 20:27)

55.   Those who blaspheme the Lord's name.
       (Leviticus 24: 15, 16)

56.   Those who are carnally minded.
       (Romans 8:6)

57.   Sodomy (oral and anal sex)
       (Genesis 19: 13, 24,25)

58.   Rebellious children.
       (Deuteronomy 21:18-21)

59.   Those who rebel against pastors.
       (Deuteronomy 17: 12)

60.   Those you curse their rulers.
       (I Kings 2: 8,9; Exodus 22:28)

Answers To Frequently Asked Questions

Q Can a Christian be cursed?

Yes. God has set a blessing and a curse before each of us – conditional, "if/then" promises. "If you will… then I will…"

(Deuteronomy 11:26-28) says:
Behold, I set before you this day a blessing and a curse; a blessing, if you obey the commandments of the Lord your God, which I command you this day: and a curse, if you will not obey the commandments of the Lord you God.

Every day, whether we know it or not, we attract curses or blessings. (Example): There are inherent problems with illegal drugs. If you buy, sell, and /or use them, you invite the demonic curses of that industry upon yourself. (The abuse of legal drugs can also invite curses.) Additionally, you'll attract the curses of potential arrest, prosecution, poverty, imprisonment, and eventually death.

If, on the other hand, you choose to live under the Lordship of Christ, and be obedient to His Word then blessings will follow your life. Blessed or cursed? The choice is yours.

Q What does the Bible say about breaking generational curses?

In *(Luke 10:19)* it says:

(Jesus speaking) "Behold, I give you the authority to trample on serpents and scorpions, and over all the power of the enemy, and nothing shall by any means hurt you."

Who are you? A born again, spirit filled Christian that knows their authority and who they are in Christ and that they have the power to come against the enemy in every area of their life – and that includes curses of every kind!

◔ Are you cursed for having an abortion?

Yes. Performing abortions is dangerous in the natural realm and very dangerous from the point of view of Scripture.

(Deuteronomy 27:25) says:
"Cursed be he that takes a reward to slay the innocent person"

(Genesis 9:6) says:
"Whoso sheds man's blood, by man shall his blood be shed."

(Exodus 20:13) says:
Thou shall not kill

Abortion is:
- Murder
- Premeditated Murder

Life does begin with conception regardless of what you may think! God's word is very clear on this subject:

(Psalm 51:5)
Behold, I was shaped in iniquity; and in sin did my mother conceive me.

(Isaiah 49:1)
The Lord hath called me from the womb; from the bowels of my mother hath he made mention of my name.

(Jeremiah 1:5)
Before I formed thee in the belly I knew thee: and before thou camest forth out of the womb I sanctified thee, and I ordained thee a prophet unto the nations.

In each of these passages we see the Lord taking action upon a person, a being, still in the womb of his mother.

What does the Bible say about sex before marriage?

(Ephesians 5:5-7)

For this you know, that no fornicator, unclean person nor covetous man, who is an idolater, has any inheritance in the kingdom of Christ and God. Let no man deceive you with empty words, for because of these things the wrath of God comes upon the sons of disobedience. Therefore do not be partakers with them.

 What does the Bible say about spiritual warfare?

(Ephesians 6:12,13)
For we do not wrestle against flesh and blood, but against principalities, against powers, against the rulers of the darkness of this age, against spiritual hosts of wickedness in the heavenly places. Therefore take up the whole armor of God, that you may be able to withstand in the evil day, and having done all, to stand.

What does the Bible say about demons?

(Luke 9:1)
Then He called His twelve disciples together and gave them power and authority over all demons, and to cure diseases.

(Luke 10:17)
Then the seventy returned with joy, saying, "Lord, even the demons are subject to us in Your name."

(James 2:19)
You believe that there is one God. You do well. Even the demons believe – and tremble!

Can Christians be demon possessed?

There is a lot of controversy about this subject – some say that a Christian can not be possessed – possession is totally taken over by a demonic force – Spirit, soul and body. People you serve the devil are possessed in all of these areas. A Christian can be oppressed, depressed, and hindered in life by demons. I believe if you give the devil any opening in your life and willfully disobey God's Word Satan will take every area of your life that you give him -- even to the point of possession!

Q What does the Bible say about demon possession/demonic possession?

(Matthew 8:28)
When He (Jesus) had come to the other side, to the country of the Gergesenes, there met Him two demon-possessed men, coming out of the tombs, exceedingly fierce, so that no one could pass that way.

Q Why does God allow Satan to attack us?

If we have legal openings or doorways (sin, ancestral curses, etc) Satan has legal right to harass and attack you. Sin must be dealt with the way God sees it from His Word. We must repent and ask forgiveness and then it is covered by the precious blood of Jesus. Then if Satan attacks you he is then trespassing.

Q Is there activity of demonic spirits in the world today?

Yes. We are surrounded by demonic activity on every turn. Television is full of evil programs full of witchcraft that you and your children see everyday! Physics and people talking to the dead is a big money maker – The toy store if full of toys that have demons attached to them and we buy them for our children and bring them into our house!!

For example: The Ouija Board goes back to the 1800's and opens a portal in the spirit world for demons to enter your life and home -- people play with this board thinking it is harmless fun and then have to have deliverance of demonic forces afterwards!!! This game is still in the toy stores today.

Q What are familiar spirits?

(Leviticus 20:27)
A man or woman who is a medium, or who has familiar spirits, shall surely be pout to death; they shall stone them with stones. Their blood shall be upon them.

(Samuel 28: 7-8)
Then Saul said to his servants, "Find me a woman who is a medium, that I may go to her and inquire of her." And his servants said to him, "In fact, there is a woman who is a medium at En Dor." So Saul disguised himself and put on other clothes, and he went, and

two men with him; and they came to the woman by night. And he said, "Please conduct a séance for me, and bring up for me the one I shall name to you."

Familiar spirit comes from a Hebrew word that suggests mumbling in a hollow sound, as a medium. This is also what we would call "channeling." Familiar spirits are demonic spirits of witchcraft that seek to possess a person who gives his/her will to them, and then imitates the voice of another or makes predictions, promotes doctrines, and so on. This spirit can continue operating within a family until it is dealt with.

Can a Christian today perform an exorcism?

As a Christian we are all called to cast out demons, but I believe you must have a direct calling from God to deal in some areas of exorcism! You can get into real trouble if you don't know what you are doing! You must be lead of God in this area!

What does the Bible say about casting out demons?

(Mark 16:15-18)
And He said to them, "Go into all the world and preach the gospel to every creature. He who believes and is baptized will be saved; but he who does not believe will be condemned. And these signs will follow those who believe: In My name they will cast out demons; they will speak with new tongues; they will take up serpents; and if they drink anything deadly, it will by no means hurt them, they will lay hands on the sick, and they will recover.

Deliverance (casting out demons) was a big part of the ministry of Jesus.

How do we distinguish a psychological disorder from demon possession?

The Bible clearly mentions the "mind of the (Holy) Spirit" and the "mind of the flesh"

(Romans 8:6)
This verse states that the mind of the flesh is "sense and reason without the Holy Spirit." It also relates the mind of the flesh to the spirit of death, which comprises all the miseries that arise from sin. Having the mind of the flesh is directly related to misery. Most of the information that we have in relation to mental illness was created from the teaching rooted in the mind of the flesh. Great minds attempt to interpret problems and give

solutions of the mind with their senses and leave the Holy Spirit out. Is mental illness demonic? I believe that more times than not – it will have demonic roots. We have decided to attempt to heal the minds of people without including the Maker and Healer of the minds. This is very dangerous, and we have paid a great price because of it. Only God can deliver, heal and restore the mind! You cannot medicate a demon – you have to cast it out!

Q Does Satan have to get God's permission before he can attack us?

Yes. Satan goes before God day and night to find something in your life that he can use against you. Having sin in your life is an opening for the enemy to attack you. And there is nothing God will do about it because you're in disobedience to God's Word. God will not violate His own word. Read *(Job 1: 6-12)* and you will see that God gave permission to Satan to attack Job – the only condition was that Satan could not kill him.

Q What are territorial spirits?

Territorial spirits are spirits that are assigned to certain areas, cities, states, etc: Satan has a well-organized kingdom.

We war against:
- Principalities
- Powers
- Rulers of darkness of this age
- Spiritual wickedness in high places

(Daniel 10: 10-13,20)
This is one of the clearest Old Testament examples that demonic armies oppose God's purposes and that earthly struggles often reflect what is happening in the heavenlies, and that prayer with fasting may affect the outcome. The prince of Persia would be the head of the spiritual forces marshaled on behalf of sinful Persia, especially in relation to its destructive interaction with God's people. Michael is a senior angel. The exact nature of the conflict and why the messenger could not defeat the prince are not stated.

The fact remains it took 21 days for the answer to get through to Daniel due to the demonic prince of Persia.

In verse 20 it states that another prince of Greece would come. Our battle is never against a person it is always against Satan and his army. We have been called to fight and we will win!

IMPORTANT: There is never anything anyone has done that God cannot forgive and bring healing in your life! If you have friends, family or anyone that is going through frustrating patterns and cycles in their life please feel free to give them this report.

*** I pray that this information has been a blessing to you and that you have discovered new revelation in the Word of God. You have purpose and destiny that God put in you from the foundation of the world – You have something to do for God!

You can experience deliverance, victory, joy and peace in God! Know that the Lord loves you and cares for you and knows what you are going through – He has given us everything we need in His Word to live a life of freedom -- it is up to us what we do with it!

THERE IS HOPE --- NEVER GIVE UP!

MAY THE LORD TOUCH YOU THIS DAY IN A VERY SPECIAL WAY AS YOU CONTINUE TO SEEK TO WALK IN OBEDIENCE TO HIM AND TO SERVE HIM!

God Bless You,

Pastor Donna Morse
Freedom Place Ministries, Inc

Declare A Thing

Job 22:28 (NKJV)
You will also declare a thing and it will be established for you so light will shine on your ways.

Hebrews 11:3
By faith we understand that the worlds were framed by the word of God, so that the things which are seen were not made of things which are visible.

Proverbs 18:20-21
A man's stomach shall be satisfied from the fruit of his mouth; from the produce of his lips he shall be filled. Death and life are in the power of the tongue, and those who live it will eat its fruit.

These scriptures are the heart and soul of decreeing the Word of God. Declaring God's Word counteracts the many words of death so often spoken without any realization of their power.

It is time to shift the tide of our lives, time to quit asking our heavenly Father to do something He has already done in Christ. It is time to **decree, proclaim and declare** the things He has already completed at the Cross.

Decree means to give an official order with the power of legislation issued by a rule or person with authority. We are simply issuing a decree, legislating with an authority given to us by God Himself to bring about His already stated divine will.

Divine Will is to make an official order, pronouncement, or legal ruling to affect something. When we speak His word, which is already established in the heavens, we enforce it through verbal agreement. Our words become the bridge linking heaven and earth. Literally speaking, we bring Heaven to earth and when Heaven is loosed in our lives or in the earth at large, things have to change.

Proclaim is to announce something publicly or formally. You have to **speak to announce.** And to what public do we announce? In the case of spiritual decrees based on the Word, we are announcing to evil forces in high places, saying, "God's word has preeminence over what we see in the natural and demand it to agree to the spoken, living Word."

Declare is to begin a fierce campaign to get rid of something or start fighting in earnest for or against something. The word fierce should get our attention. We are informed the kingdom of heaven suffers violence and the violent take it by force *(Matthew 11:12).* Other words for fierce are: violent, ferocious, brutal, vicious, and aggressive like the anger of a guard dog and with intensity. When we declare over another life the heart and Word of God we are like a guard dog on their behalf. In the case of declaring against injustice there are to be no holds barred in our brutal, vicious assault on the enemy.

Time and Effort

You may be asking yourself how many times, how often, or how long I should decree. The simple answer is, "Until it is manifest or the Holy Spirit speaks clearly and releases you."

Decreeing, proclaiming or declaring is not something we pick up and do once in a while. We do it till we see the answer, the fruit. We do it till we can pick up the juicy fruit and bite into the ripeness of sweet success. We do it until we can eat of it, share it, and fill the earth *(**Genesis 1:28**)*.

One caution I would give you is this; do not be dismayed or be discouraged when decreeing starts to feel in any way as if you are doing it by a fixed routine or repetition. This is one of the biggest ploys of the enemy to get you off track, to stop you in your tracks. When we buy into this lie we begin to believe there is no power because we are just mouthing words. This is not possible seeing the Word has its own inherent power because it is living. We are not just mouthing words; we are releasing power no matter how it looks or feels. Consistency is the key, NOT FEELINGS!

Remember, God's Word does not return void and He watches over His Word to perform it *(**Isaiah 55:11 Jeremiah 1:12**)*. In other words, it is His job to bring it to pass and your job to release the Word into your life by declaring, decreeing and proclaiming. The Word's power is not based on how we feel, think, or anything else, because it is living and is endued with inherent power by God. What a freeing principle this is, knowing we could never, ever do it right enough! All we have to do is speak in agreement and He performs it!

Reality of Life in the Earth Today and God's Remedy

You and I both know it is so very easy to speak negative words, focus on negative aspects, and believe everything will always be the same. At every turn we are bombarded with negative news and hopelessness intended to rob our hope. We all know if we speak adverse words over someone's life long enough they will embrace those words as being who they are. As a result, death is created. The purpose, the beauty of who God says they are is robbed. If not corrected, goes on for generations to come, with increase. There is a better way!!

The world we live in today can only be transformed by one person, Jesus Christ and His Word. How else will the Word of God be loosed into the earth, into our families unless we speak it?

The scripture tells us God framed the worlds with His words and we are created in His image *(Hebrews 11:2-4) Gen 1:27)*.

Since we are created in His image, He expects us to be like Him in what we say, thereby, framing our own world around us with our words too.

He has given us an abundance of building blocks in the Word and we can choose to use them or not, to speak life or not. Regardless of which we choose to do, speak life or speak death, the Word is clear. We will eat the fruit produced by our labors, our words.

God's Word is His will and you are brought into alignment with His will when you speak His Word. There is no other way. There are not shortcuts!! But there are incentives, promises and rewards to those who do not grow weary in doing good.

You may be asking, "Do I have to speak it out loud?"

The answer is "Yes!" And why?

Because everything God ever did was done with words. Reflect back over creation and remember how many times He said, "Let there be!" The words "spoke and speak" are used over 1400 times in the New King James Version. Obviously speaking has great relevance and power!

Everywhere you turn, people are spewing negative, critical words of death, totally unaware or unwilling to look at the consequences of their words. Much is done out of habits learned and taught in homes. **It is time for a change, time of a transformation to take place. It is time to be fruitful, multiply, take dominion and fill the earth with His glory, to fill the earth with His word.**

It Is Time For Us To See Our Own Personal Lives Transformed

(Genesis 1:28)

Transformations will come because we speak His will, His living Word over our lives, and this will bring about change in the world around us, filling it with the manifestation of Christ. **It MUST AND WILL START WITH OUR LIFE FIRST. IT ALL STARTS WILL YOU!**

Father, in the name of Jesus, I decree and declare:

I decree and declare that all generational spirits that came into my life during conception, in the womb, in the birth canal, and through the umbilical cord to come out in the name of Jesus. I break all spoken curses and negative words that I have spoken over my life in the name of Jesus. I break all spoken curses and negative words spoken over my life by others, including those in authority in the name of Jesus.

I decree and declare that all ancestral spirits of freemasonry, idolatry, witchcraft, false religion, polygamy, lust, and perversion to come out of my life in the name of Jesus. I command all hereditary spirits of lust, rejection, fear, sickness, infirmity, disease, anger, hatred, confusion, failure, and poverty to come out now in the name of Jesus.

I decree and declare that the legal rights of all generational spirits operating behind a curse are broken in the name of Jesus. You have no legal right to operate in my life from this day forward. I bind and rebuke all familiar spirits and spirit guides that would try to operate in my life from my ancestors in the name of Jesus. I renounce all false beliefs and philosophies inherited by my ancestors in the name of Jesus.

I decree and declare that all curses on my finances from any ancestors that cheated or mishandled money are broken in the name of Jesus. I break all curses of sickness and disease and command all inherited sickness to leave my body now in the name of Jesus. I renounce all pride inherited from my ancestors in the name of Jesus. I break all oaths, vows, and pacts made with the devil by my ancestors in the name of Jesus. I break all curses by agents of Satan spoken against my life in secret in the name of Jesus.

I decree and declare that all written curses that would affect my life are broken in the name of Jesus. I break every time-released curse that would activate in my life as I grow older in the name of Jesus.

A time-released curse is a curse that has a right to abide in a person's life because of a hook in the soul. This hook in the soul, which is the actual incident that causes the suppression; (It is the willful or unconscious pressing down of things below the level of consciousness. When a person pushes things deep down inside, it is like putting trash in a trash compactor. Though it is formed into a nice, neat, little package at the bottom of the container, it is still there and will eventually begin to stink. Foul, unclean spirits of suppression lie dormant in the lives of people for years!!) has a right to come out of hiding as a result of an omen or prognostication (to foretell from signs or symptoms) of a demon called **Father Time.** Father Time has a stopwatch to assure that the timed-release curse is ignited in the demonic time set. When people suppress things in their lives, they appear to have victory in an area of their lives until **Father Time** says. "Time is up --- the suppression must manifest itself now! – and it will manifest itself when you least expect it. Just as emotions can be suppressed, so too can demons be suppressed. Demons can lie dormant and be activated by **Father Time.** Whether it is **emotional, mental, or demonic suppression**, the hook must be removed so that the devil can have not part in us.

I break and take authority over the bondage of all **suppression**, and I now remove all the **demonic, mental and emotional hooks** out of my soul in the name of Jesus so that the devil can have no part in me. I now bind the strongman of **Father- Time** off of my life from this day forward. I break the cycle of time-released curses off of my life and that the stopwatch will no longer be ignited by the demonic time set. I command all foul, unclean spirits of suppression that are lying dormant in my soul to now be exposed and come to the light of the Holy Spirit. Soul, you will no longer willfully or unconsciously press or hide things below my level of consciousness.

I decree and declare that all demonic spirits of arrested development that denies any growth in my life to come out in the name of Jesus. I command and break all demonic spirits of revolt and rebellion against the laws of God. I command all cruelty that has crushed my emotions and the flow of God in my life to make it rocky and filled with bondages broken in the name of Jesus. I command and break all that breeds a false strength and causes demonic coping to hide the true inner weakness in my life in the name of Jesus. I command and break the demonic root of pride and rebellion in the name of Jesus.

I decree and declare that every curse of Balaam hired against my life is broken in the name of Jesus. Lord, turn every curse spoken against my life into a blessing. I break all generational rebellion that would cause me to resist the Holy Spirit.

I decree and declare that all spirits of oppression and the harsh burdensome weight of heaviness is broken off of my mind with the tormenting spirits of cruelty now in the name of Jesus. I bind the strongman of the taskmaster that rules over my head in tyranny. I command and break the spirit of the slave that is upon me that causes me to not have rule over my spirit. I command and break the strength of natural and spiritual slavery that weighs and oppresses me down under a load on my back. I command and break the spirit of infirmity off of my back now in the name of Jesus. I now remove the load of the taskmaster from my back in the name of Jesus. I break and destroy the **reins of the yoke** that connects me to the reins that guide my life. I command the yoke off of my neck to be broken and destroyed now in the name of Jesus. I command and cut the sprits of pride and deception loose from one another that have yoked themselves together with all oppressive spirits to keep me under the rule of the taskmaster without me being aware of it now in the name of Jesus.

I bind the spirit of heaviness in the name of Jesus!

I decree and declare that every false covering that would make my mind weary and the spirit despondent to go in Jesus' name. I break the curse of the "sleep of death" and decree that in my darkest nights I have hope that joy is coming in the morning. I command the sun to be my friend and not my enemy. I will rise up and let the enemies of my soul be displaced… forever! Every devil of heaviness, suicide, give up, and can't take it anymore --- you lie down and die!! I will live and not die. The walking dead is sent back to the caverns of hell to be tormented. You have failed in your assignment. It is legal and official --- **Your Assignment Of Depression And Heaviness Is Broken Forever!**

I decree and declare that the powers of darkness are broken off my mind, right now in Jesus name! I command the light to be strong in my eyes so that my body can be whole. Let the light come! I command the darkness of depression and the confusion of anxiety to go! Every psychosomatic disorder that has affected my life must bow to the blood of Jesus.

Every psychic attack, physical attack, spiritual attack, social attack, emotional attack, financial attack, or material attack is bound and blocked forever in Jesus name. The residue from trauma is dried to the roots, and the wounds are healed, down to my literal spirit man. The anointing destroys every yoke in my life …. in Jesus name. I command the poison that the arrows have injected into my wounds through trauma to come out now in the name of Jesus and all spirits of bondage relating to the killing effects from the tainted arrows must leave my life now in the name of Jesus!

I decree and declare that all spirits of fear, torment, anxiety and panic attacks are leaving me now in the name of Jesus. I come against fast heart rate, shortness of breath, obsession, fear of dying, equilibrium imbalance and insomnia. I bind the strongman of Pan and I command all pandemonium, chaos, confusion, mental anguish, and insanity to leave me now in the name of Jesus.

I decree and declare that all demonic assignments over my life and the lives of my family are broken and canceled out now in the name of Jesus. I command the spirit of death and destruction broken off of my life from this day forward in Jesus name. I bind the strongman of death, the Grim Reaper off of my life and your assignment is null and void in the name of Jesus.

I decree and declare that the demonic threefold cord of pride is broken now in the name of Jesus. I sever Leviathan (neck) Behemoth (Loins) and Cockatrice (mind) one from another. I take the sword of the Spirit and I cut them loose from each other now in the name of Jesus. I sever the agreement of the strongmen and break all cords between them and cast them out now in the name of Jesus. I command all pride, error, deception, false religion, illusion, delusion, every mind blinding spirit to loose me and come out now in the name of Jesus. I command and call out lofty self-respect, self-satisfaction, self-importance, overbearing spirit, disdain, arrogant attitude, presumption, haughty spirit, extreme selfishness, exaggerated faith in self you must leave my life now in the name of Jesus. I break and command all bondage in the neck, the loins, and the mind to be broken and to leave me now in the mighty name of Jesus Christ.

I decree and declare that all spirits of **insecurity** (the state of being not secure, not confident, not firm) and **inferiority** (the state of feeling lower in position, stature, or value) are broken this day in the mighty name of Jesus Christ.

Father, in the name of Jesus, I decree and declare:

That my spirit man is clad with the armor of the Lord and the armor of light.

That Your kingdom is my priority and Your assignment is my pleasure. Let Your kingdom come and Your will be done on earth as it is in heaven.

I function and conduct my life's affairs according to Your original plan and purpose for me.

I walk in Your timing.

You are the one and true God, who makes everything work together and who works all things for good through Your most excellent harmonies. Cause my will to work in perfect harmony with Yours.

Evil shall not come near my dwelling, since I dwell in the secret place of the Most High God and dwell under the shadow of the Almighty.

I cause demonic, destiny-altering activities to cease. I take hold of the ends of the earth and shake evil out of its place.

I break evil and inappropriate thought patterns in my mind.

I speak peace into my life, relationships, ministry, workplace, and business.

Everything that is misaligned I command to come into divine alignment.

I have the mind of Christ and therefore seek things above and not beneath.

I ascend into new realms of power and authority and access new dimensions of divine revelation.

I will not backslide or look back into old ways, old methodologies, or old strategies unless directed by You to do so.

I wear the helmet of salvation to protect my mind from negative thoughts that would derail Your purposes and plans for me.

Truth protects my integrity, righteousness protects my reputation, the gospel of peace guides my every step, the shield of faith secures my future and destiny, and the sword of the Spirit grants me dominion and authority.

I decree and declare a prophetic upgrading of my thought life. I cancel the affect of negative, self-defeating thought processes and patterns and put them under my feet.

I possess a kingdom paradigm, which grants me new ways of thinking, new ways of working, and new ways of living.

New cycles of victory, success, and prosperity will replace old cycles of failure, poverty, and death in my life.

I now have a new, refreshed, cutting-edge kingdom mentality.

At Your Word, as a kingdom trailblazer, I pioneer new territory.

Everything that pertains to my life and godliness and everything prepared for me before the foundation of the world must be released in its correct time and season. I command everything to be released now in Jesus' name.

I decree and declare that there will be no substitutes, no holdups, no setbacks, and no delays.

Since Your Word is a lamp unto my feet and a light unto my path, I shall neither stumble nor fall.

I am excited; my spirit is ignited; I walk in favor with God and man.

I am a success-oriented individual, and everything I touch turns to "prophetic gold".

I am a successful business owner—an entrepreneur who provides good jobs to others.

Today I am blessed, there is no lack, all my needs are met, I am out of debt, and I have more than enough to give over and above all my needs.

All financial doors are opened, and all financial channels are free. Endless bounty comes to me.

Sufficient is Your provision for today.

I am healed and Spirit filled; sickness and disease are far from me.

I have buying power on my dollar, and I live in prosperity.

I confess that I only progress; I experience no setbacks and live a life filled with success.

I will persist until I succeed.

I walk in dominion and authority. My life is characterized by liberty.

There is no slackness in my hand. Where I stand God gives me the land.

The blessings of the Lord make me rich, and I am daily loaded with benefits.

I am living my most blessed and best days now.

I am crowned with God's love and mercy. With all good things He satisfies me.

My home is a haven of peace.

I do my work as unto the Lord with diligence and in the spirit of excellence.

My home, business, departments, and ministries function smoothly and efficiently.

The Lord gives me wisdom, knowledge, and understanding as to how to do my work more effectively, professionally, and accurately.

The Lord gives me all the right people to work with and for me. Together we work as unto the Lord.

Relationships will come to me that are assigned to enhance my life and ministry for this season.

I call forth every individual and resource assigned to assist me in the fulfillment of my kingdom assignment during this season.

I attract only the things, thoughts, people, and resources suitable to undergird and facilitate God's original plan and purpose for my life.

I am favored by all who know me, meet me, work with me, and have any kind of formal or informal relationship with me.

I will work with You as my partner. I work according to Your daily agenda and perform for an audience of one----the Lord Jesus Christ.

My work is my worship.

You are teaching me how to improve my productivity --- to work smarter and more efficiently.

I always function with an outstanding attitude and produce superior work.

You empower me to make positive and significant deposits in other people's lives.

I seek divine opportunities and occasions to help others succeed.

I maximize my potential and move boldly toward my destiny.

I am a purpose-driven, kingdom-principled, success-oriented individual, and I refuse to be distracted by insignificant things and people.

Let favor, well wishes, ambassadorial courtesies, kindness, and support be extended to me by all who are assigned to me, meet me, know me, and interact with me.

I do no procrastinate. I act now, without hesitation, anxiety, of fear.

I excel in all things, at all times, with all people, under every circumstance.

I am fruitful.

I have power to gain wealth.

Wherever I go, systems, institutions, cultures, environments, legislation, codes, ordinances, regulations, and policies adjust to accommodate my divine purpose.

I am adaptable and flexible and make needed adjustments.

I am in the perfect place for You to bless me.

My relationships are fruitful and mutually beneficial.

I am celebrated and loved by all who come in contact with me.

Everything about me is changing for the best.

I am healthy and physically fit.

Sickness and disease are far from me.

My mind is fortified and resolute.

My emotions are sound and stable.

My faith is steadfast and unfaltering.

The zeal of the Lord fills my soul and spirit.

Let there be no demonic encroachment. Let there be no satanic squatters – in the name of Jesus, get off my property, get off my territory, get out of my sphere of influence, get out of my family, get out of my relationships, get out of my finances, get out of my body, and get out of my mind.

I command mountains to be removed and to be cast into the sea.

I am gaining new territories: new emotional territory, new intellectual territory, new business territory, new ministerial territory, and new financial territory.

I decree and declare this day that the Son of God was manifested to destroy the works of the devil to the very depths of hell. And in this moment, I loose the manifestation of

Jesus, the Son of God, tearing to pieces every design of the devil in the kingdom of darkness over my life.

I pray right now for God's plans to prosper in my life and I pull down, from Heaven to earth, everything God has designed for my life right now in the name of Jesus Christ! Father, I wait to see Your finished product. I look forward to the day that I will be transformed into the image of Your dear Son. My heart's deepest desire is to be like Him.

I seal these declarations in the name of Jesus, my Lord and Savior. Now unto Him that is able to do exceeding abundantly above all that I could ask or imagine, according to the power that works in me: to Him that is able to keep me from falling and to present me faultless before the presence of His glory with exceeding joy, and to sustain my body, soul, and spirit; to the almighty God my heavenly Father, the King eternal, immortal, invisible – the only wise God – be honor and glory forever and ever.

(Spend sometime in praise and thanksgiving knowing that God has heard and will respond)

Hallelujah!... I PRAISE YOU, GOD... Amen!